DA
ZHIMINGDE

STRIKING DEADLY BLOWS TO VITAL ORGANS

MASTER HEI LONG

PALADIN PRESS
BOULDER, COLORADO

Other books by Master Hei Long:
Advanced Dragon's Touch: 20 Anatomical Targets
    and Techniques to Take Them Out
Dragon's Touch: Weaknesses of the Human Anatomy
Gouzao Gongji: Seven Neurological Attacks
    for Inflicting Serious Damage
Guge Gongji: Seven Primary Targets
    to Take Anyone Out of a Fight
Iron Hand of the Dragon's Touch: Secrets of Breaking Power
Master's Guide to Basic Self-Defense: Progressive Retraining
    of the Reflexive Response

Da Zhimingde: Striking Deadly Blows to Vital Organs
by Master Hei Long

Copyright © 1993 by Master Hei Long

ISBN 10: 0-87364-700-9
ISBN 13: 978-0-87364-700-7
Printed in the United States of America

Published by Paladin Press, a division of
Paladin Enterprises, Inc.
Gunbarrel Tech Center
7077 Winchester Circle
Boulder, Colorado 80301 USA
+1.303.443.7250

Direct inquiries and/or orders to the above address.

PALADIN, PALADIN PRESS, and the "horse head" design
are trademarks belonging to Paladin Enterprises and
registered in United States Patent and Trademark Office.

Visit our Web site at www.paladin-press.com

CONTENTS

WARNING

The techniques and drills depicted in this book are extremely dangerous. It is not the intent of the author or publisher to encourage readers to attempt any of these techniques and drills without proper professional supervision and training. Attempting to do so can result in severe injury or death. Do not attempt any of these techniques or drills without the supervision of a certified instructor.

The author and the publisher disclaim any liability from any damage or injuries of any type that a reader or user of information contained within this book may encounter from the use of said information. This book is *for information purposes only.*

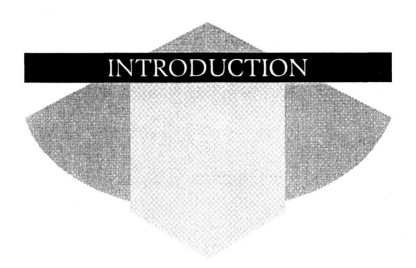

INTRODUCTION

Da Zhimingde is the third and final phase of a three-part study in which seven primary targets were categorically selected for each phase, then analyzed for their anatomical locations and their physiological functions and weaknesses. Guge Gongji was a study of locomotion, the axial and appendicular skeletons, and the structure, function, and relative weaknesses of each joint according to its posture. Gouzao Gongji studied neurological targets, analyzing the effects of striking them from a physiological and combative perspective.

The targets of Guge Gongji were selected with the goal of structural immobilization in mind. Those of Gouzao Gongji were chosen to bring about neural immobilization. The targets of Da Zhimingde differ greatly from those of the two previous works.

The literal translation, "Striking Deadly Blows," typifies the mechanics of Da Zhimingde. Da Zhimingde is primarily a study that focuses on vital sensory and life-support organs, the majority of which are lethal when attacked properly.

It is logical—and necessary—to study all three phases in this series. To use the techniques of Guge Gongji against an opponent who presents only a minimum of danger would be unnecessarily brutal. Using the techniques of Da Zhimingde against a dangerous, but not lethal, opponent would be similarly unjust.

By design, the techniques of Da Zhimingde are to be used when your life or your health are in serious jeopardy. Keep this in mind as you pursue the study.

CHAPTER ONE
The Seven Primary Targets

The seven primary targets upon which this study will focus are named and exhibited in their anatomical locations in Figures 1 through 3. First, however, a final word about the physiological nature of this set of targets is in order.

The targets of Da Zhimingde, for the most part, are *lethal*. The *fossa temporalis*, carotid plexus, and anterior neck region are the most potentially fatal of the seven. The heart and kidneys follow, in that order. The eyes and groin, though not lethal targets, are serious ones, the former being the more so of the two.

It is by design, not coincidence, that the targets of Da Zhimingde are lethal. These are the targets you aim for when your life or health is seriously threatened. Knowing them well may allow you to spare a life if you have reason to . . . or take one if necessary.

Target Number 1: *Fossa Temporalis*
The *fossa temporalis* is among the deadliest targets. Substantial force of impact and accuracy are necessary when striking this target, but, given these factors, a blow to this area is lethal. This is a combination target area which will require some explanation.

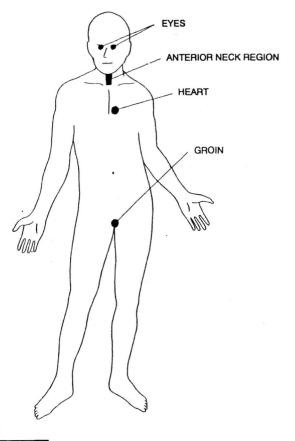

figure 1

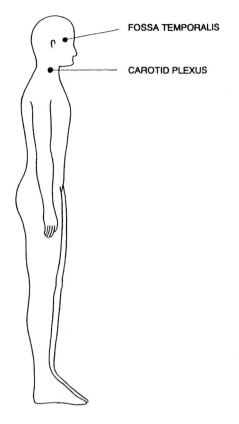

FOSSA TEMPORALIS

CAROTID PLEXUS

figure 2

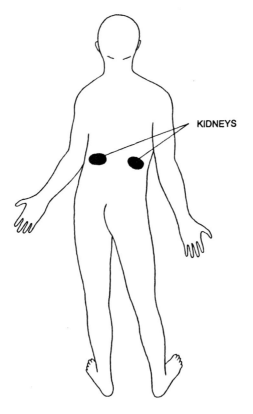

KIDNEYS

figure 3

Observe Figure 4. This is the sphenoid—a bone within the cranium, situated toward the anterior section of the skull horizontally and about halfway down vertically. The areas denoted in the illustration are the great wings, the small wings, and the tips of the great wings. The tips of the great wings surface at the blackened area in Figure 5 and meet the corresponding bones of the skull. The sphenoid also assists in forming the plate upon which the bulk of the brain rests within the skull.

Reach up with your left hand and, using the tips of the second and third fingers, press into the temple area. Observe Figure 6. The middle meningeal artery is responsible for the pulse you detected with your fingertips. This

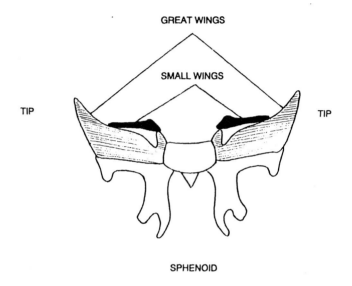

GREAT WINGS

SMALL WINGS

TIP   TIP

SPHENOID

figure 4

artery, which is the longest branch supplying the dura mat-
ter, passes outside the tips of the great wings of the sphenoid, rising through the zygomatic arch. When the *fossa
temporalis* is attacked, there are two possible consequences,
each of which poses a threat to life. A blow of high impact
focused directly into the depression of the temple will trap
the meningeal artery between the weapon and the tip of
the wing of the sphenoid. The bursting artery will cause
lethal compression of the brain. Secondly, a deep, pene-
trating high-impact blow will have the effect noted above
but can also snap the tip of the great wing, forcing the
splintered bone into the brain.

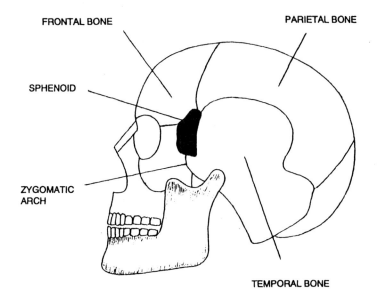

figure 5

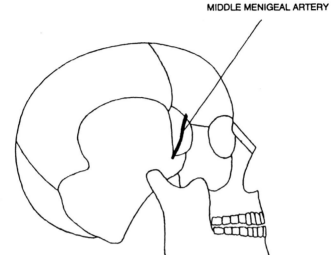

MIDDLE MENIGEAL ARTERY

figure 6

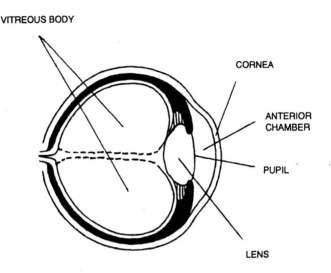

figure 7

Target Number 2: Eyes

The eyes are, for the most part, a target of strategy and availability. Any direct contact with the eyes will cause the eyelids to slam shut and the lacrymal gland to secrete fluid across the eyeballs. This uncontrollable reaction, termed "conjunctival reflex," was discussed in detail in *Master's Guide to Basic Self-Defense* (available from Paladin Press). Because of the sensitivity of the eyes, this target is most valuable in close-contact fighting, when powering up a blow with distance and multiple power sources through rotation is not feasible.

The basic structure of the eye is depicted in Figure 7. The lens, pupil, and anterior chamber are covered by a transparent tissue called the cornea, which blankets the

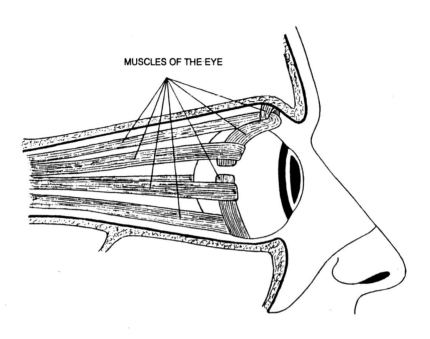

MUSCLES OF THE EYE

figure 8

entire eyeball. As the illustration depicts, the bulk of the eye consists of the vitreous body—two fluid-filled chambers.

Figure 8 shows the muscles of the eye and its position in the skull. Only one-sixth of the eyeball is exposed, while the remaining portion is held deep within the orbital fissures by the corresponding muscles and the fascia bulbi (the fatty substance that holds the eye snugly within the orbit).

Brushing across the eye with a finger or fingernail will cause pain, watering, and temporary visual dysfunction. Poking an eye will cause extreme pain, watering, and temporary dysfunction. A deep poke into an eye can cause it to be ejected from its socket or, if the vitreous body is ruptured, to collapse.

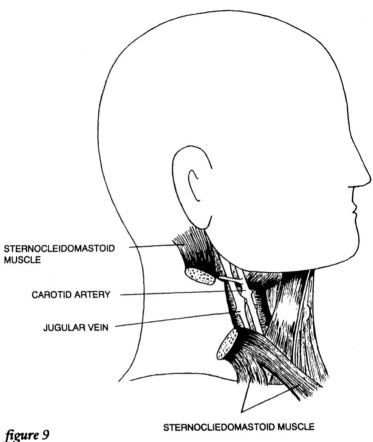

STERNOCLEIDOMASTOID
MUSCLE

CAROTID ARTERY

JUGULAR VEIN

STERNOCLIEDOMASTOID MUSCLE

figure 9

Target Number 3: Carotid Plexus

The carotid plexus is formed by the carotid artery and the jugular vein. It ascends from the aorta and supplies blood to the brain through each of its two branches. The jugular vein, which itself has a branch on each side of the neck, returns blood from the brain to the heart via the superior vena cava. The muscle that covers the carotid plexus, the sternocleidomastoid muscle, is acutely sensitive, as are the smaller muscles behind the plexus.

Observe Figure 9. The sternocleidomastoid muscle has been sectioned to illustrate the position of the carotid plexus. The jugular vein and the carotid artery lie very closely together beneath the muscle and can therefore be struck simultaneously.

The effects of damaging the carotid plexus will be instantaneous. Dizziness followed by unconsciousness will be the first response to a high-impact blow to the area. Also, the carotid plexus supplies the majority of the brain's blood supply, and, as with the damage to the meningeal artery that occurs in an attack on Target Number 1, compression of the brain is the result of interrupting its blood flow.

Considering the effects noted above, and the pain and spasms from striking the sternocleidomastoid muscle, the carotid plexus is a target you should seek when circumstances dictate a "serious threat" type of confrontation.

Target Number 4: Anterior Neck Region

No other area of the human anatomy is more vulnerable to attack than the anterior neck region. Two functions of the body are absolutely crucial to life: the intake and expulsion of air and the circulation of blood. Stop either of these and the body begins to expire immediately. (By design, the body operates these two systems without requiring the conscious activity of the brain. Otherwise, of course, you would die in your sleep. Though you can take conscious control of your breathing, as soon as you release that control, the brain once again maintains a normal breathing pattern.) A properly executed blow to the anterior neck region will cause breathing to cease.

Observe Figure 10. The esophagus is a collapsible tube through which solid and liquid nutrients ingested orally enter the digestive system. It is approximately 10 inches long and extends from the pharynx through the diaphragm and the abdominal cavity into the stomach. Its location within the thorax follows the path depicted in the illustration: behind the trachea and the heart.

The trachea is the air passage leading directly into the lungs. Positioned in front of the esophagus, the tracheal tube is held in its cylindrical shape by tiny, C-shaped hyaline cartilages, allowing for the free passage of air into and out of the lungs.

The larynx is the communicating passage between the trachea and the esophagus. Assisted by the thyroid carti-

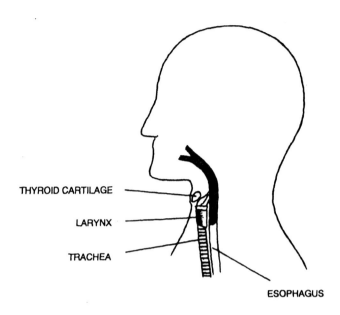

THYROID CARTILAGE

LARYNX

TRACHEA

ESOPHAGUS

figure 10

lage (Adam's apple), the larynx regulates the passage of air and nutrients into the appropriate tubes.

These sensitive passages, covered only by a layer of skin, are virtually unprotected until they descend below the level of the sternum. A high-impact blow into the trachea will break the hyaline cartilage, which will puncture the soft tissue, sending blood down into the lungs. Damage to the thyroid cartilage or the larynx will cause this vital airway to collapse, resulting in asphyxiation.

Target Number 5: Heart

As mentioned above, the flow of blood is the second bodily function that is crucial to maintaining life. There is

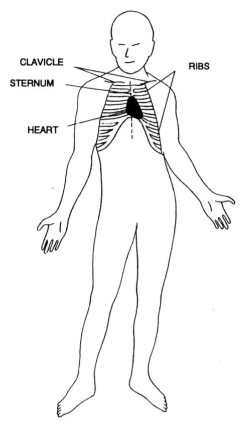

CLAVICLE

STERNUM

RIBS

HEART

figure 11

one central organ in the body responsible for maintaining the flow of blood: the heart. When the heart stops, life stops.

Unlike the anterior neck region, the heart is well protected, encased within the bony, articulated structure called the thorax, which is comprised of the ribs and sternum. Without passing either under or through the rib cage, it is impossible to make direct contact with the heart. But this target can be affected by a properly placed, properly delivered blow.

Observe Figure 11. The clavicle supports the span of the shoulders and provides a stabilizing connection for the superior end of the sternum. The sternum functions as the anterior connecting point for the ribs, binding their ends

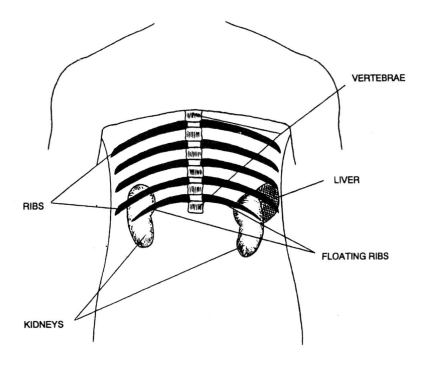

figure 12

with cartilaginous joints to close the thorax over the heart. The communicating thoracic vertebrae form the dorsal connection for the ribs As the illustration shows, the heart rests behind the distal portion of the sternum, the bulk of it leaning to the left of the centerline (depicted by the dotted line).

Deep-penetration blows will jar the heart, of course, but controlled-penetration concussion blows are the most effective against this target. Effective attacks to the heart will cause instantaneous unconsciousness; the perfected concussion blow is lethal.

Target Number 6: Kidneys

The kidneys function primarily to collect water and

waste products from the bloodstream, create urine, and excrete it into the bladder. The body's blood supply is pumped through the renal artery into the kidneys, where the chemical end products of metabolism are removed, maintaining the delicate homeostatic balance of body fluids. If the kidneys fail to function properly, the resulting cell changes that occur within the bloodstream will poison and eventually kill the afflicted person.

Observe Figure 12. Note first that the right kidney is slightly more exposed than the left. This is because of the close proximity of the liver, which pushes the kidney downward. Resembling lima beans in shape, the kidneys measure approximately four and a half inches in length, two to three inches in width, and about one inch in thickness. Connective tissues and fatty cushions hold them in their anatomical positions.

Striking the kidneys with high-impact blows causes excruciating, crippling pain, and should the organ rupture on impact, death would be the probable result. If you will notice, the last two ribs (floating ribs) end over the kidneys. The ends of the other 11 pairs are bound by cartilage. If one of these "floating" ribs is hit with enough force to break it off, forcing it into the kidney, the effect would be the same as thrusting a knife into the organ.

Target Number 7: Groin

An anatomical analysis of the groin is not necessary, nor is a discussion of its sensitivity. The organ is a preferable target because of its sensitivity to pain, as well as its accessibility.

The anatomical location of the groin at the bottom of the centerline makes it more vulnerable to attack than other targets. During a physical confrontation, the hands are generally held at about chin level. Consequently, blocking a blow to the head, neck, or chest requires only a minimum of movement. Because of the groin's distance from the bulk of the most vital areas, blocking it requires a lengthy movement, making it more difficult to defend effectively.

CHAPTER TWO
Directions of Force

In studying directions of force, note that, as a rule of thumb, the impact force will almost always follow a perpendicular line into the target. That is, the most effective incoming blow will approach the target at a right angle, as opposed to approaching it along a plane that would result in a glancing blow. There are exceptions to every rule, and this one has its variables as well. But in seeking the optimum effect from your hand strikes or kicks, the line of force is a crucial factor, and you would do better to follow the direct-line (right angle, perpendicular) rule unless your familiarity with the target dictates otherwise.

As you study the targets, envision the strikes you would use on each. If an angled direction of force is taught, fix it in your mind and train your attacks to that target accordingly.

Target Number 1: *Fossa Temporalis*

The straight-line punch, focused backhand, palm-up and palm-down sutos, hand hammer, hook kick, and roundhouse kick are all excellent weapons to use against the *fossa temporalis* (fig. 13). Blows to this area should follow a perpendicular line aimed to pass directly through the opposing temple, as depicted by the arrows in Figure 14.

figure 13

The straight-line punch and sutos are the most effective weapons against this target because their striking surfaces are small and will enter the depression of the temple, making surface contact with the middle meningeal artery.

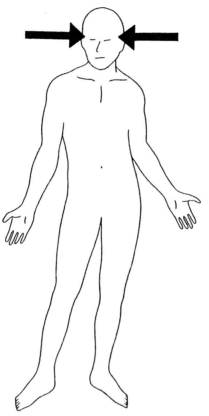

figure 14

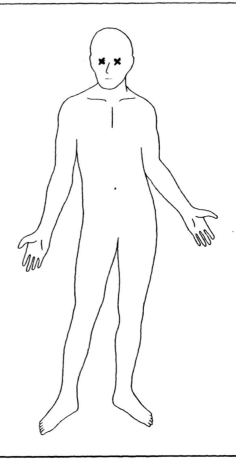

figure 15

Target Number 2: Eyes

Single-finger, two-finger, and claw strikes work best for attacks to the eyes because their striking surfaces fit right into the orbital fissures (fig. 15). The roundhouse kick and hook kick also work well but with less efficiency. If you are barefoot or wearing soft-bottom shoes, the heel of a side kick will make fair contact with the eyes. The arrow in Figure 16 depicts the preferred direction of force, but a push or scrape at any angle will be effective.

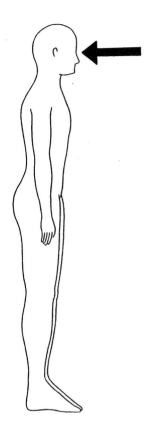

figure 16

figure 17

Target Number 3: Carotid Plexus

The roundhouse and hook kicks are excellent weapons against the carotid plexus (fig. 17) because their drive lines finish on a horizontal plane, as indicated by the arrows in Figure 18. Sutos and hand hammers also work well on this target, and the length of the artery and vein comprising the carotid plexus offers a degree of latitude with the precision.

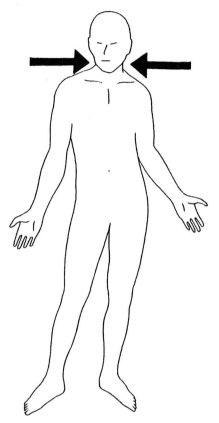

figure 18

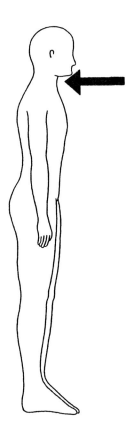

figure 19

Target Number 4: Anterior Neck Region

Your straight-line strokes (fig. 19), with approximately three inches of penetration, are the best weapons to use against this target (fig. 20). The side kick works well when you are facing your opponent, while roundhouse and hook kicks are the most effective when the opponent is positioned to your side.

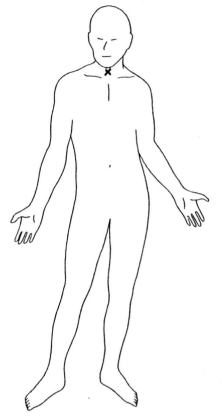

figure 20

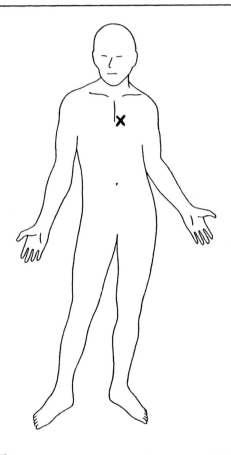

figure 21

Target Number 5: Heart

The half-turn punch is the first-choice hand strike for the heart (fig. 21). When the opponent's body is in the proper position, the roundhouse is the first-choice kick. The palm strike (especially circular), hand hammer, and elbow strikes are effective upper-body weapons against the heart, and the front, heel-thrust, and side kicks are your best lower-body weapons. Whichever weapon is used to attack this target, the blow should follow the angle of force indicated by the arrow in Figure 22.

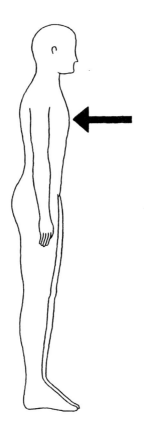

figure 22

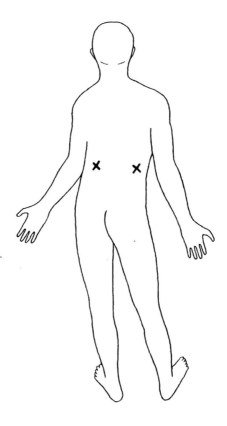

figure 23

Target Number 6: Kidneys

Straight punches, hand hammers, side kicks, hook kicks, and roundhouse kicks all work well against the kidneys (fig. 23). Observe Figure 24. The angle indicated by arrow A will focus the force of impact on bursting the kidney; a blow that follows the angle indicated by arrow B will drive the twelfth rib down into the organ. A slightly inclining blow will also work well against the kidney, but with a lesser effect.

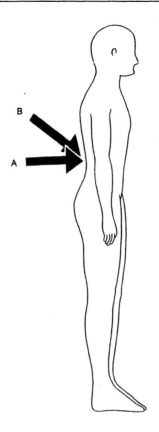

figure 24

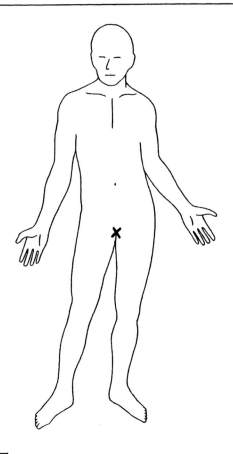

figure 25

Target Number 7: Groin

For attacks against the groin (fig. 25), whether hand strikes or kicks, the angle of arrow A in Figure 26 is the preferred direction of force. The angle of arrow B will work, but it is not as effective. Front kicks and circular, rising palms are the most effective weapons against the groin, but heel thrusts, side kicks, punches, and backhands also work well.

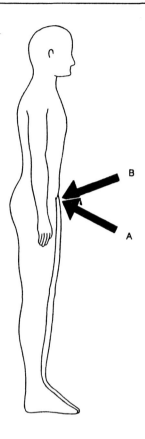

figure 26

CHAPTER THREE

Single-Kick Returns

The remaining four chapters of this text will focus on the practical application of our target studies—that is, attacking the seven primary targets of Da Zhimingde with a variety of single and combination strokes, using both kicks and hands strikes. Because the targets—and their vulnerability—are central to Da Zhimingde, accuracy should be a focal point in training with these movements.

As you practice the following techniques, recall the locations and physiology of the targets you are striking. All of these counterattacks will target the pressure points analyzed in the first two chapters.

Figures 27 through 31

Figure 27. In this technique, you (black-striped shorts) will target the groin with a low front kick. You'll use an inside suto block with an arm trap and maintain your grip through the execution of the kick. Your opponent will be approaching your north gate. Figure 27 is your starting position.

Figure 28. Flatten your right foot, shifting your body weight onto the corresponding leg. Note that this short step not only facilitates the kick, but also adds distance

figure 27

between you and the incoming punch your opponent has initiated from his right side.

Figure 29. Stop the incoming punch with an inside suto block.

Figure 30. Rotate your blocking hand outward, taking a grip on your opponent's wrist and bringing it down to the position shown for control. As you do this, shift your weight onto your right leg and chamber a left front kick.

Figure 31. Maintaining your grip on your opponent's arm, snap your chambered kick into his groin.

figure 28

figure 29

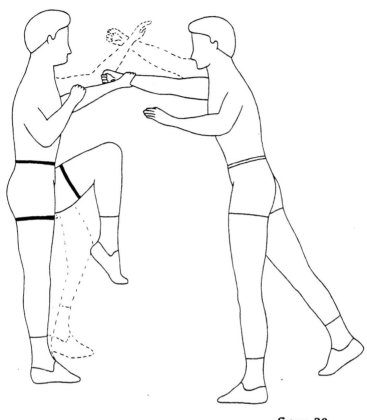

figure 30

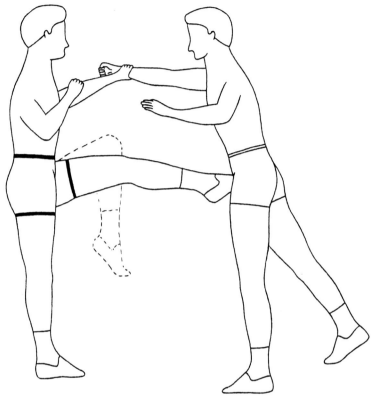

figure 31

figure 32

Figures 32 through 36

Figure 32. In this sequence, you're going to attack the same target with a different kick. Pay close attention to the chamber and extension positions of this kick as opposed to those of the previous one.

Figure 33. Shift your body weight onto the right leg and take a short step back with your left foot.

Figure 34. Stop the incoming blow with an inside suto block.

Figure 35. Rotate your blocking hand outward, taking a grip on your opponent's punching arm at the wrist and bringing it down to the position shown for control. As you

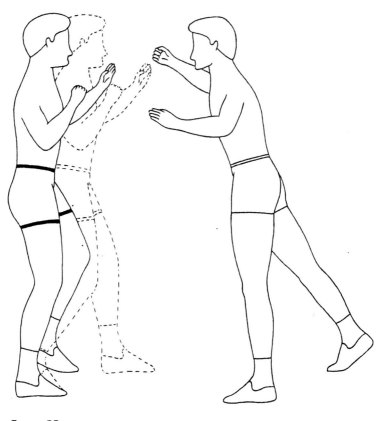

figure 33

do this, shift your weight onto your right leg and chamber your left heel-thrust kick.

Figure 36. Retaining the grip on your opponent's arm, lock your heel-thrust kick into your opponent's groin.

figure 34

figure 35

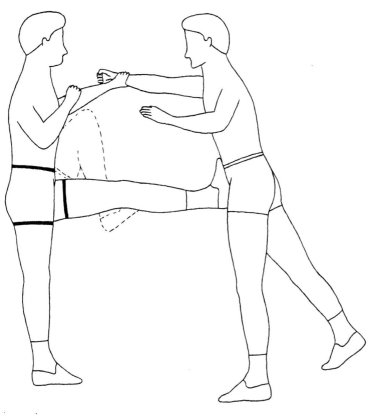

figure 36

figure 37

Figures 37 through 41

Figure 37. In this sequence, we will apply the heel-thrust kick to a higher anatomical target. The block and chamber positions remain unchanged from the previous technique; only the height of the kick will change.

Figure 38. Shift your body weight onto the right leg and take a short step back with your left foot.

Figure 39. Stop the incoming blow with an inside suto block.

Figure 40. Rotate your blocking hand counterclockwise and take a grip on your opponent's punching arm at the wrist. Bring the arm down and toward you as shown, while simultaneously chambering your left heel-thrust kick.

figure 38

Figure 41. Lock your heel-thrust kick out into your opponent's heart.

figure 39

figure 40

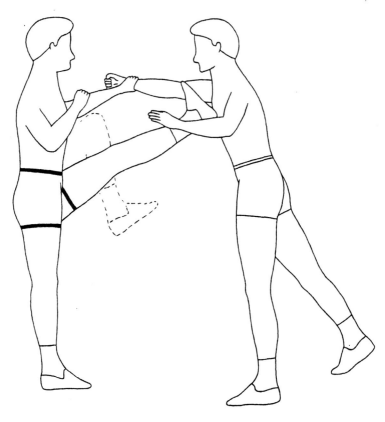

figure 41

figure 42

Figures 42 through 46

Figure 42. In this technique, we are going to change weapons and targets. Coming from the same block and adjusting step, you will chamber a roundhouse kick and direct it at the carotid plexus.

Figure 43. Set your right heel down, shifting your body weight onto the corresponding leg, and step back with the left foot as illustrated.

Figure 44. Stop the incoming punch with an inside suto block.

Figure 45. Rotate your blocking hand outward, taking a firm grip on your opponent's wrist. Pivot counterclockwise

figure 43

to 90 degrees on the left foot and chamber a right round-house kick.

Figure 46. Extend your roundhouse kick into your opponent's carotid plexus.

figure 44

figure 45

figure 46

figure 47

Figures 47 through 51

Figure 47. Here you will use the same adjusting step, block, chamber, and kick, but you are going to raise the kick a few inches from the previous target and strike the *fossa temporalis*.

Figure 48. Set your right heel down, shifting your weight onto the corresponding leg, and step back with the left foot to the position shown.

Figure 49. Stop the incoming punch with an inside suto block.

Figure 50. Rotate your blocking hand outward, taking a firm grip on your opponent's wrist. Pivot counterclockwise

figure 48

to 90 degrees on the left foot and chamber your right roundhouse kick.

Figure 51. Snap your kick up and into your opponent's *fossa temporalis*.

figure 49

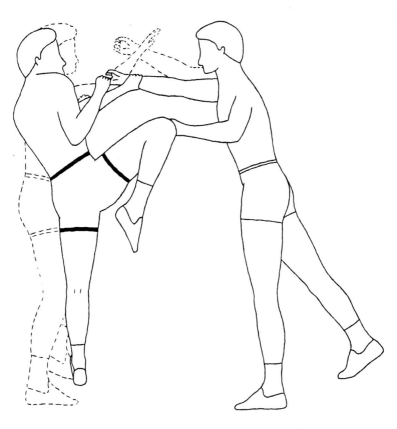

figure 50

figure 51

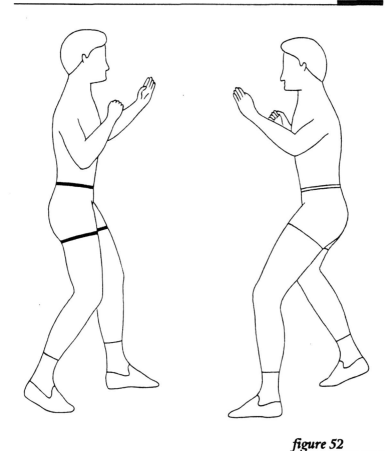

figure 52

Figures 52 through 56

Figure 52. Though we will continue to utilize the adjusting step, inside suto block, and 90-degree pivot, we will change chamber positions and kicks in this technique.

Figure 53. Shift your body weight onto the right foot and take a short adjusting step back with your left foot.

Figure 54. Stop the incoming punch with an inside suto block.

Figure 55. Rotate your blocking hand outward, taking a grip on your opponent's punching arm at the wrist and pulling it down as shown. Simultaneously pivot to 90 degrees and chamber your right leg for a side kick.

Figure 56. Thrust your side kick into your opponent's

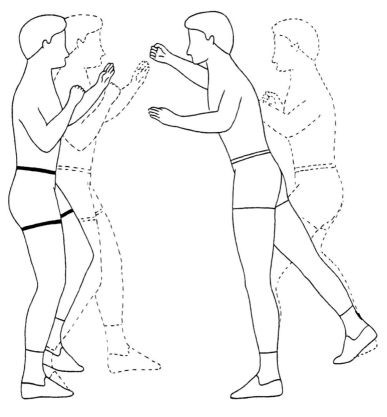

figure 53

heart. Note that in this technique you release the opponent's trapped arm to allow for the full extension of the
kick.

figure 54

figure 55

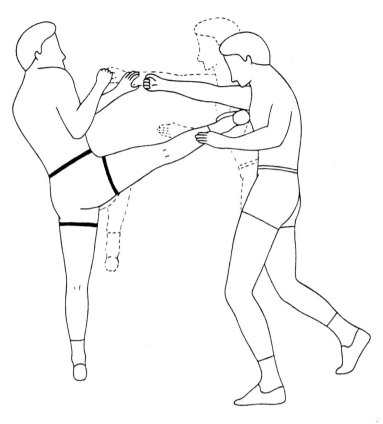

figure 56

figure 57

Figures 57 through 61

Figure 57. The adjusting step, block, chamber position, and kick will not change in this technique, but we attack a higher and certainly more deadly target: the anterior neck.

Figure 58. Shift your body weight onto the right foot while taking a short adjusting step back with your left foot.

Figure 59. Stop the incoming punch with an inside suto block.

Figure 60. Rotate your blocking hand outward, taking a grip on your opponent's punching arm at the wrist and pulling it down as shown. Simultaneously pivot to 90 degrees and chamber your right side kick.

figure 58

Figure 61. Thrust your side kick upward into your opponent's anterior neck region.

figure 59

figure 60

figure 61

figure 62

Figures 62 through 66

Figure 62. This final block and return sequence follows the pattern of the previous technique, but there is a minor height/target adjustment in the kick.

Figure 63. Shift your body weight onto the right foot while taking a short adjusting step back with your left foot.

Figure 64. Stop the incoming punch with an inside suto block.

Figure 65. Rotating your blocking hand outward, take a grip on your opponent's punching arm at the wrist and pull it down, while simultaneously pivoting to 90 degrees and chambering your right side kick.

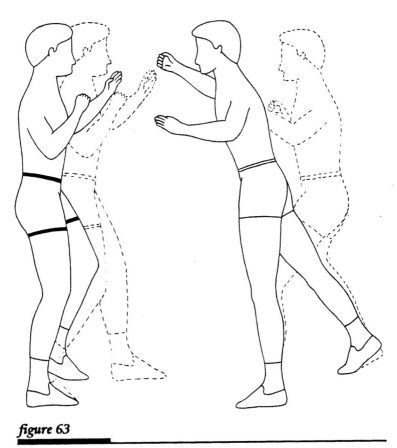

figure 63

Figure 66. Thrust your right side kick upward into your opponent's eye.

figure 64

figure 65

figure 66

figure 67

Figures 67 through 78

In the next 12 illustrations, we are going to study the roundhouse kick, applied offensively against an opponent who is facing you from a side-straddle stance. Note the gaps between you and your opponent in the starting frames for each sequence. The targets being attacked will progress in height with each new sequence, beginning with the groin and ending with the *fossa temporalis*.

In practicing these kicks, concentrate on moving from your starting position through the extension of the kick in one smooth, flowing effort. The chamber position is not a stopping point, but an intermediate, transitional position used to guide the kick in its proper path toward the target.

figure 68

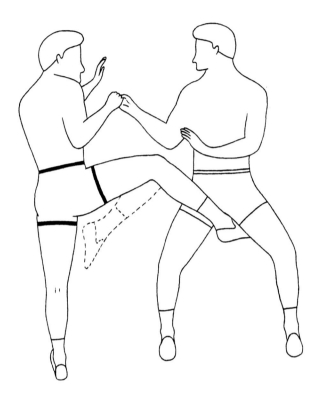

figure 69

figure 70

figure 71

figure 72

figure 73

figure 74

figure 75

figure 76

figure 77

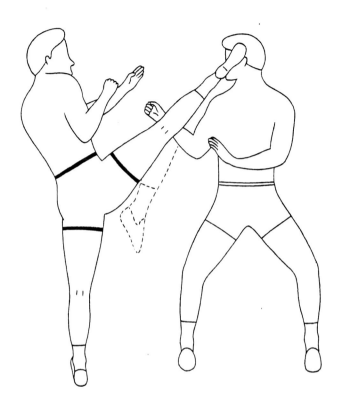

figure 78

CHAPTER FOUR

Single-Punch Returns

The array of hand weapons used in the martial arts provides a variety of instruments with which to strike anatomical targets. From the more dense weapons, such as punches and hand hammers, to the narrower, acicular formations, such as the claw, tiger mouth, and straight finger, hand strikes have the inherent value of having a higher potential for precision application of force, especially against smaller, receded targets. Hand techniques are also quicker than kicks due to the lesser distance they are required to travel to reach the extended position.

Work for accuracy in these techniques. One precisely delivered blow is better than three sloppily thrown, inaccurate strikes.

Figures 79 through 82

Figure 79. In this first technique, we are going to use an inside suto block with a grapple and return a horizontal palm-up suto. Pay special attention to the lean in the last frame.

Figure 80. Your opponent has leaned forward and initiated a wide right roundhouse punch.

Figure 81. Meet the incoming punch with a left inside

figure 79

suto block, and chamber your right hand to the high suto position.

Figure 82. Three movements occur in this frame: your blocking hand grapples the offending arm, you lean slightly forward to accommodate the appropriate striking distance, and you have struck the *fossa temporalis* with a horizontal palm-up suto.

figure 80

figure 81

figure 82

figure 83

Figures 83 through 86

Figure 83. The movements of this technique are a near carbon copy of our previous one, but we are going to place the strike on a slightly lower target this time: the carotid plexus.

Figure 84. Your opponent leans forward and initiates a wide right roundhouse punch.

Figure 85. Meet the incoming blow with a left inside suto block, and chamber your right hand to the high suto chamber position.

Figure 86. Again, three movements transpire here. Your blocking hand grapples the opponent's punching arm, you lean slightly forward to accommodate the appropriate

figure 84

striking range, and you strike your opponent's carotid plexus with a horizontal palm-up suto.

figure 85

figure 86

figure 87

Figures 87 through 90

Figure 87. The technique we will study here is designed for simplicity, speed, and effectiveness. From a wide right roundhouse punch, we will use the inside suto block and a straight-line claw strike to the eyes.

Figure 88. Your opponent leans forward and initiates a wide right roundhouse punch.

Figure 89. Stop the incoming punch with a left inside suto block. Do not move the right hand. Your return strike comes directly from the ready position.

Figure 90. Form your hand into the claw position and, in a tight, straight line, snap it into your opponent's eyes.

figure 88

figure 89

figure 90

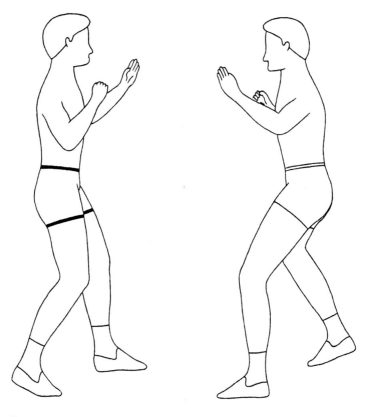

figure 91

Figures 91 through 94

Figure 91. We will again use an inside suto block against a wide right-handed punch, followed by a straight-line, open-hand return strike.

Figure 92. Your opponent leans forward and initiates a wide right roundhouse punch.

Figure 93. Meet the incoming punch with a left inside suto block, holding the right hand in its present position.

Figure 94. Form a straight weapon with your right hand and, in a tight, straight line, snap it into your opponent's anterior neck region.

figure 92

figure 93

figure 94

figure 95

Figures 95 through 98

Figure 95. In this technique, we will work with a different punch and block, and we'll return a concussion punch to the heart.

Figure 96. Your opponent initiates an advance with a straight-line punch aimed at your center gate.

Figure 97. With a scooping palm block, deflect the incoming punch outside the width of your body.

Figure 98. Snap out a right half-turn punch to your opponent's heart.

figure 96

figure 97

figure 98

figure 99

Figures 99 through 102

Figure 99. Using the same block and punch studied in the previous technique, we will return a horizontal hammer blow to the carotid plexus. Pay attention to the gap adjustment in the last frame.

Figure 100. Your opponent initiates an advance with a straight-line punch aimed at your center gate.

Figure 101. Using the scooping palm block, redirect the punch beyond the width of your body and chamber your high right suto.

Figure 102. With the same circular motion the palm-up suto uses, throw a palm-up vertical hammer to your opponent's carotid plexus.

figure 100

figure 101

figure 102

figure 103

Figures 103 through 106

Figure 103. We are going to change the block, the sides of the body, and the return strike in this sequence. Be sure to observe the illustrations closely.

Figure 104. Your opponent begins an advance with a center-gate, straight-line punch.

Figure 105. As the punch nears, use a right palm block crossing your body and deflect the blow outside the width of your body on the left side.

Figure 106. With the left hand, snap out a straight fore-fist strike to your opponent's anterior neck region.

figure 104

figure 105

figure 106

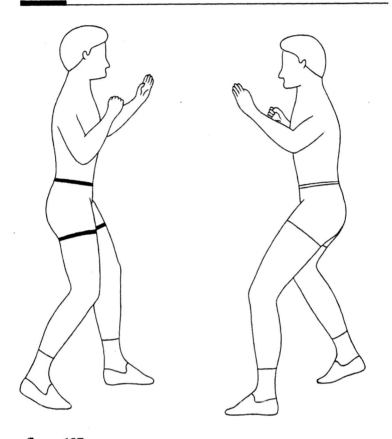

figure 107

Figures 107 through 110

Figure 107. Changing blocks again, we will block a high-gate punch and return a different hand strike.

Figure 108. Your opponent advances with a high-gate, straight-line punch.

Figure 109. With your left hand, redirect the incoming punch across your body outside the right shoulder while taking a short outside step. Drop the right hand as shown.

Figure 110. Slap the groin with a rising palm strike.

figure 108

figure 109

figure 110

figure 111

Figures 111 through 114

Figure 111. In this last sequence, we will use the same block but with a straight-line return strike.

Figure 112. Your opponent again advances with a high-gate, straight-line punch.

Figure 113. Taking your outside step, deflect the incoming punch with a left crossing palm block. Keep the right hand in its ready position.

Figure 114. Open your right hand and snap a tiger mouth strike into your opponent's anterior neck region.

figure 112

figure 113

figure 114

CHAPTER FIVE
Combination Kicks

Combinations—whether with kicks, hand strikes, or a miscellany of both—must be characterized by continuity and a smooth, flowing motion. Choppy, sluggish movements will complicate the delivery and effectiveness of the techniques.

Mastery of combinations begins with mastering the individual movements, and such is the result of practice. You have already performed the kicks used in these combinations by training the single block and return techniques in Chapter 3. When these single returns become comfortable, familiar movements, you will be ready to study the combinations.

Figures 115 through 121

Figure 115. From a high right roundhouse punch, you will stop the incoming blow with a left inside suto block and, using your left foot, return a front kick to the groin and a heel-thrust kick to the heart.

Figure 116. As your opponent initiates his punch and forward motion, take a short step with your left foot to adjust your distance from the blow.

Figure 117. Stop the incoming blow with a left inside suto block.

figure 115

Figure 118. Rotate your blocking hand outward and take a firm grip on your opponent's wrist. Simultaneously chamber your left leg for a front kick.

Figure 119. Snap your front kick into your opponent's groin.

Figure 120. From the groin kick, chamber your leg for a heel-thrust kick.

Figure 121. Thrust your heel kick into your opponent's heart.

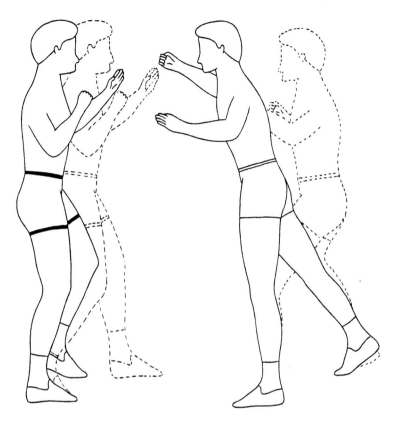

figure 116

figure 117

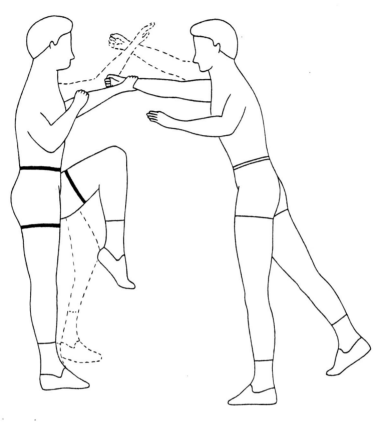

figure 118

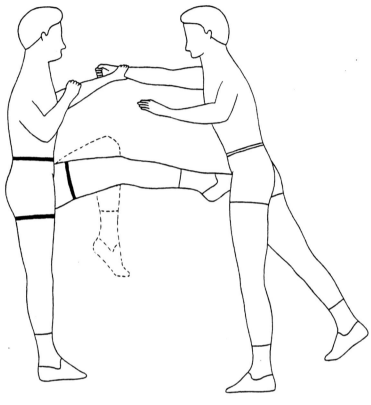

figure 119

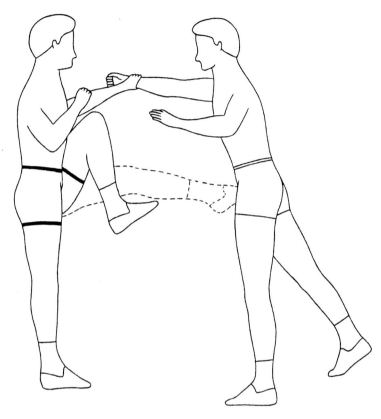

figure 120

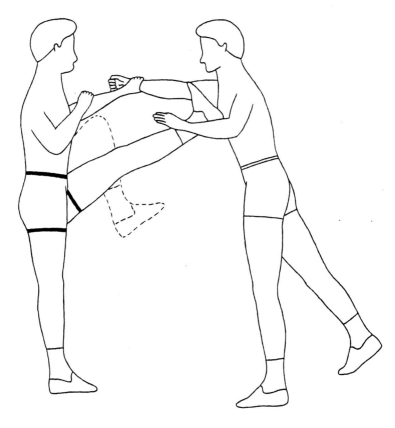

figure 121

figure 122

Figures 122 through 128

Figure 122. Changing legs in a combination kick at close proximity can be accomplished with a step and pivot or a hop. In this technique, we are going to follow a left kick with a right kick, using a hop to chamber the second.

Figure 123. As your opponent begins his wide right-hand punch advance, take a short step back with your left foot as shown.

Figure 124. Stop the incoming punch with an inside suto block.

Figure 125. Take a full grip on the offending arm at the wrist and chamber your left foot for a front kick.

figure 123

Figure 126. Snap your front kick into your opponent's groin.

Figure 127. From the position in Figure 126, push off with your right foot, rotate your body in the air, and land on your left foot with your right foot chambered for a high roundhouse kick.

Figure 128. Snap your roundhouse kick up and into your opponent's *fossa temporalis.*

figure 124

figure 125

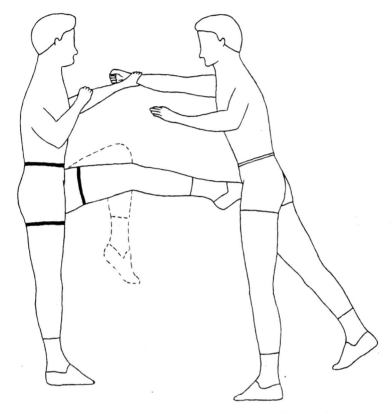

figure 126

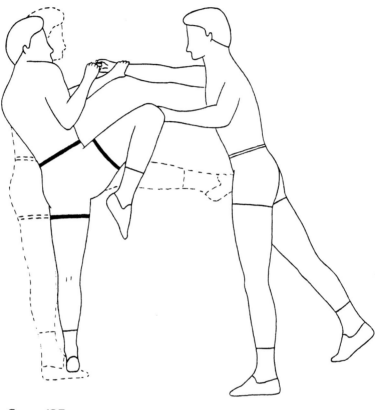

figure 127

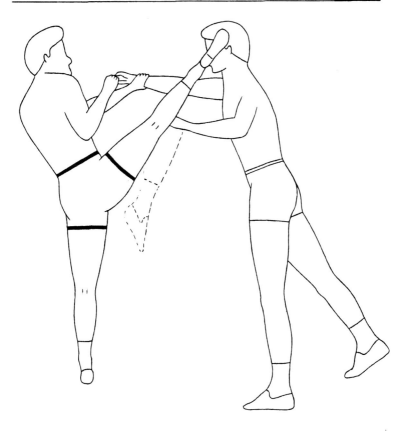

figure 128

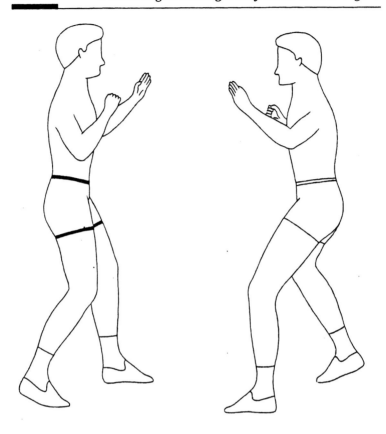

figure 129

Figures 129 through 135

Figure 129. The combination in this sequence will incorporate the same pair of return kicks, but you will seek a different target with your second kick.

Figure 130. The incoming punch is again a wide right roundhouse punch aimed at your high vertical gate.

Figure 131. Stop the incoming punch with a left inside suto block.

Figure 132. Rotate your blocking hand outward and take a full grip on the offending arm at the wrist while chambering your left foot for a front kick.

Figure 133. Snap your chambered front kick into your opponent's groin.

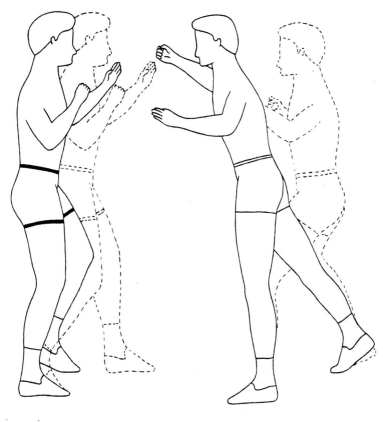

figure 130

Figure 134. As in the previous technique, hop onto your left foot at the angle shown and chamber your right roundhouse kick.

Figure 135. Extend your roundhouse kick into your opponent's carotid plexus.

figure 131

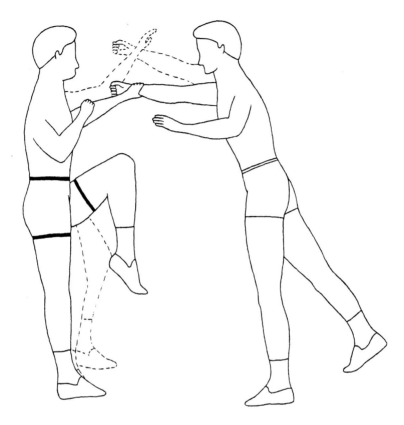

figure 132

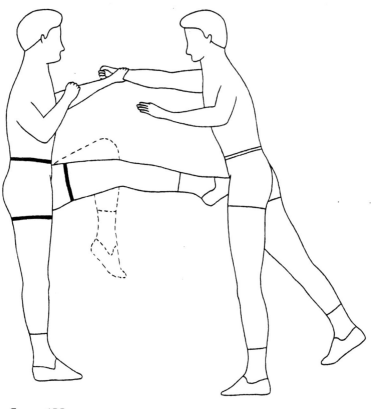

figure 133

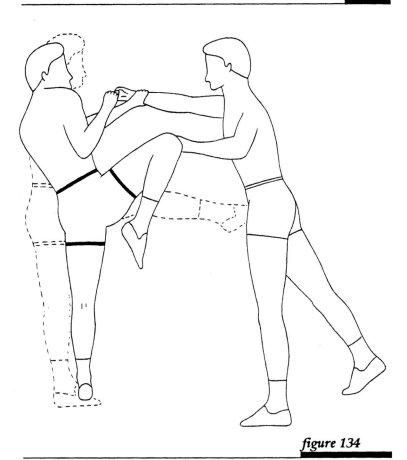

figure 134

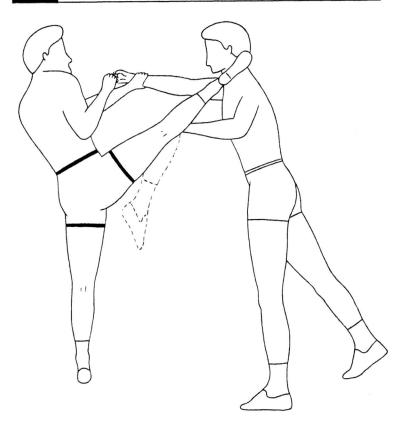

figure 135

figure 136

Figures 136 through 142

Figure 136. Both of your kicks will come off the same leg in this combination: a side kick to the heart and a roundhouse kick to the *fossa temporalis*.

Figure 137. As your opponent initiates his punch and forward motion, take a short step back with your left foot to increase your distance from the incoming blow and adjust your kicking range.

Figure 138. Stop the incoming blow with a left inside suto block.

Figure 139. Take a full grip on the opponent's arm at the wrist, shift your body weight onto the left foot, pivot to 90 degrees, and chamber your right side kick.

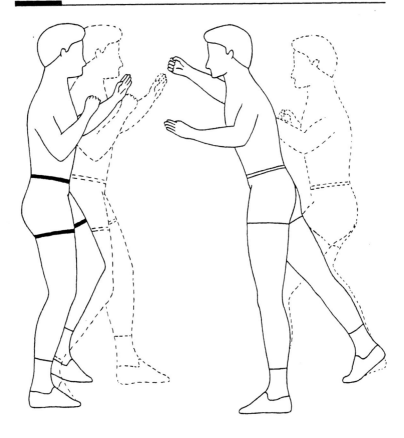

figure 137

Figure 140. Lock your side kick into your opponent's heart. According to the length of his arm, you may have to shorten the kick to maintain your grip on his arm and keep him in place for the next kick.

Figure 141. Retract your side kick and rechamber for a right roundhouse kick.

Figure 142. Complete the combination by snapping out a roundhouse kick to your opponent's *fossa temporalis*.

figure 138

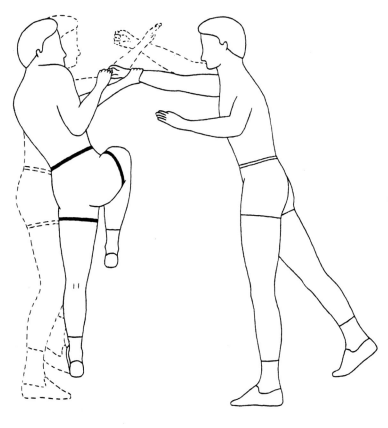

figure 139

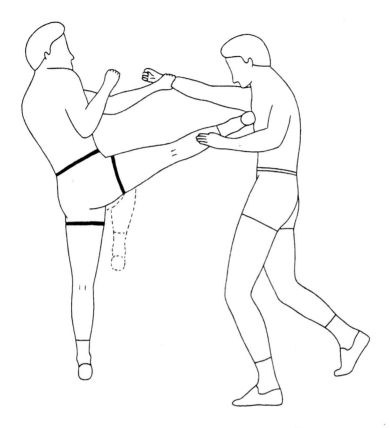

figure 140

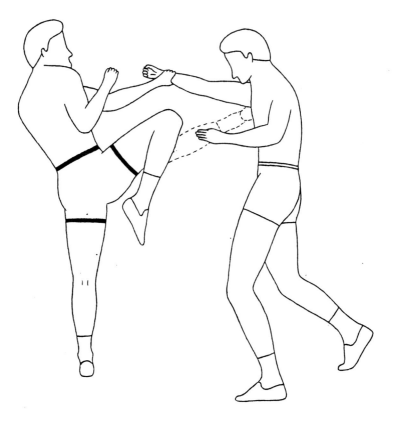

figure 141

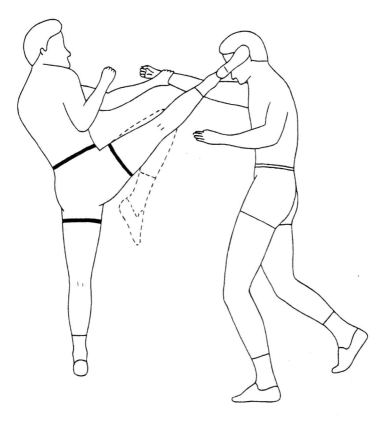

figure 142

figure 143

Figures 143 through 149

Figure 143. In this last technique, we will use two consecutive side kicks in combination: one to the heart and one to the anterior neck region.

Figure 144. Make your left rear adjusting step as your opponent initiates his forward punching motion.

Figure 145. Stop the incoming punch with a left inside suto block.

Figure 146. Shift your weight onto the left foot and pivot to 90 degrees. Grasp the punching arm firmly at the wrist and chamber your right side kick.

Figure 147. Lock your side kick into your opponent's heart.

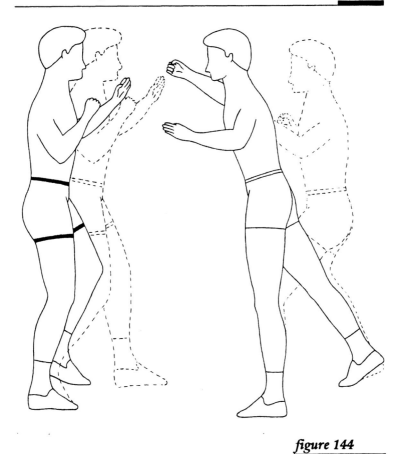

figure 144

Figure 148. Retract your kick and rechamber for another side kick.

Figure 149. Lock your side kick into your opponent's anterior neck region.

figure 145

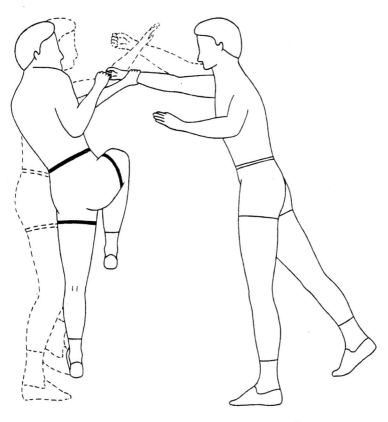

figure 146

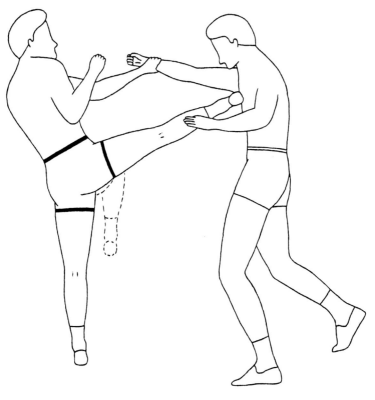

figure 147

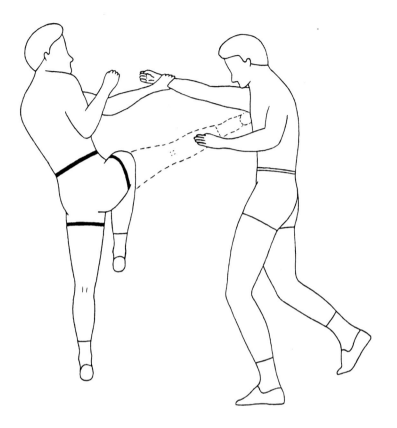

figure 148

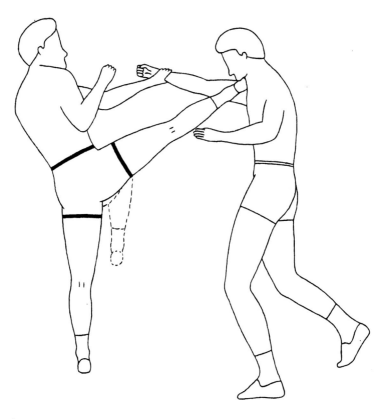

figure 149

CHAPTER SIX

Hand Combinations

As was discussed at the beginning of Chapter 5, to be effective, combinations must be characterized by fluid transitions from move to move. Absolute physical familiarity with the movements is necessary, but fluidity also comes from what we call effortless effort: the ability to move at high speed without strain, the ability to generate crushing power without strain. This, again, is the result of serious, concentrated practice. Only through repetition can one master the techniques of any physical art. The decision as to the level of skill to be achieved rests with the practitioner.

Figures 150 through 155

Figure 150. In this technique, we will use a forefist and suto combination from a rising palm block.

Figure 151. Your opponent advances with a center-gate, straight-line half-turn punch.

Figure 152. With a crossing palm block, redirect the incoming punch outside the width of your body.

Figure 153. Form a forefist with the left hand and snap it into your opponent's anterior neck region. Note the extension of the striking arm. By relaxing the shoulder and

figure 150

rolling it forward, you can add approximately six inches of reach to your strike.

Figure 154. Bring the left hand down, taking a full grip on your opponent's striking arm, and chamber your right hand at the high suto position.

Figure 155. Strike your opponent's *fossa temporalis* with a horizontal palm-up suto.

figure 151

figure 152

figure 153

figure 154

figure 155

figure 156

Figures 156 through 161

Figure 156. Using an outside palm block, we will deflect a high, straight right punch and return a rising palm and a close-range palm-up suto.

Figure 157. Your opponent advances with a high straight-line punch.

Figure 158. Deflect the incoming punch with a left palm block, while simultaneously stepping outside its path. Drop your right hand to the position shown.

Figure 159. Lean forward, guiding the offending punch outside your right shoulder and strike the groin with a rising palm slap.

figure 157

Figure 160. Retract the palm strike to the high suto chamber position.

Figure 161. Push the opponent's arm down and out of your way, and throw a horizontal palm-up suto, targeting the carotid plexus.

figure 158

figure 159

figure 160

figure 161

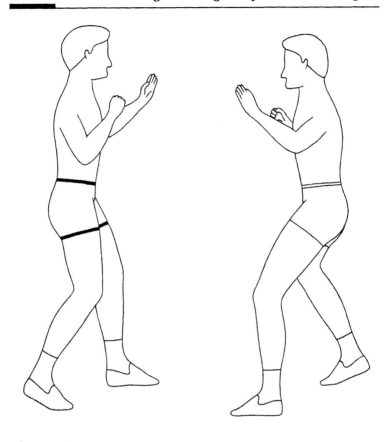

figure 162

Figures 162 through 166

Figure 162. We will change blocks again in this technique and use two closed-hand return strikes: a palm-up hammer and a straight-line half-turn punch.

Figure 163. Your opponent advances with a center-gate, straight-line half-turn punch.

Figure 164. Deflect the punch with a left scooping palm block and bring your right hand to the high suto chamber position.

Figure 165. Strike your opponent's carotid plexus with a horizontal palm-up hammer fist. As you extend your hammer strike, bring your left hand to the chin chamber position.

figure 163

Figure 166. Throw a straight-line half-turn punch to your opponent's heart. Bring your right hand back to the ready/chamber position as you extend the punch.

figure 164

figure 165

figure 166

figure 167

Figures 167 through 171

Figure 167. Starting from the center-gate punch and scooping palm block used in the previous technique, we will return two straight-line strokes: one to the heart and one to the anterior neck region.

Figure 168. Your opponent advances with a straight-line half-turn punch directed to your center gate.

Figure 169. Redirect the punch outside the width of your body with a left scooping palm block.

Figure 170. Strike your opponent's heart with a right, straight-line half-turn punch, while bringing the left hand to the chin/chamber position.

figure 168

Figure 171. Using a straight-finger thrust, strike your opponent's anterior neck region.

figure 169

figure 170

figure 171

figure 172

Figures 172 through 176

Figure 172. Going back to the inside suto block, we will block a high roundhouse punch and return two open-hand strikes: a straight-finger thrust and a claw strike.

Figure 173. Your opponent initiates a high, wide round-house punch aimed at your upper gate.

Figure 174. Stop the incoming blow with a left inside suto block.

Figure 175. Extend a right straight-finger thrust to your opponent's anterior neck region. Form your left hand into the claw position as you lock out your first strike.

Figure 176. Extend your claw strike into your opponent's eyes.

figure 173

figure 174

figure 175

figure 176

figure 177

Figures 177 through 181

Figure 177. In this final technique, we will defend against an opponent in a side-straddle stance using a left lunge punch.

Figure 178. From his side-straddle position, your opponent lunges forward, initiating a half-turn punch to the center gate.

Figure 179. Deflect the incoming punch outside the width of your body with a left scooping palm block.

Figure 180. Take a short forward shuffle step and drive a palm-up punch into your opponent's left kidney. As you deliver the punch, form the left hand into the claw position.

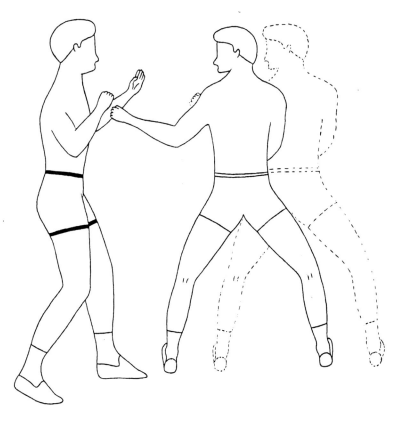

figure 178

Figure 181. Snap your claw strike into your opponent's eyes and return your right hand to the ready/chamber position.

figure 179

figure 180

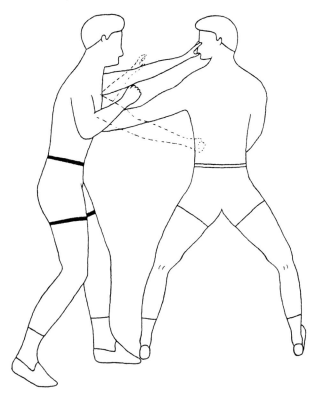

figure 181